nintendogs™

Do You Know Your Dog?

A Breed-by-Breed Guide

by Dr. Dog as told to Howie Dewin

SCHOLASTIC INC.

New York   Toronto   London   Auckland   Sydney
Mexico City   New Delhi   Hong Kong   Buenos Aires

ISBN 0-439-84367-7

TM & © 2006 Nintendo
Used under license by Scholastic Inc. All rights reserved.
Published by Scholastic Inc. SCHOLASTIC and associated logos are trademarks and/or registered trademarks of Scholastic Inc.

12 11 10 9 8 7 6 5 4 3 2   6 7 8 9 10/0

Printed in the U.S.A.
First printing, April 2006

Taking care of a dog means a lot more than just a good scratch behind the ears. Trust me, I should know. I'm Dr. Dog, and you know what that means.

I'm not just a doctor.

I'M A DOG.

So I know, first paw, what it takes to be a first-rate dog care provider. You have to think about food and exercise, grooming and training, socializing and obedience. But the trickiest part is that you have to do all this for someone you can't understand. If humans would only learn to bark, the world would be a simpler place.

But since you don't bark and we don't speak Human, I will tell you what I tell my patients: "If you want to stay happy and healthy, then you have to get your caretaker to think like a dog."

That means the first thing YOU have to do is learn about dogs. Then you can start figuring out just what your dog needs and wants. Of course, every dog is different. But certain dogs have similar traits, and that's what I'm going to tell you about now. I've organized this book by types of dogs.

Or, as I like to say: "It's on a breed-to-know basis."

So scratch your ear with your foot and curl up on the couch with this book. Before you know it, you'll be thinking like a dog!

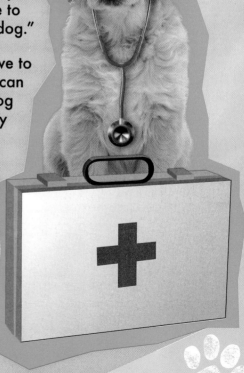

Miniature Pinscher

Average height:
9 3/4 to 11 3/4 inches
Average weight:
8 to 11 pounds
Coloring:
various shades of brown

Origins: I'm from Germany, where *pinscher* means "biter." (By the way, I am *not* a miniature Doberman Pinscher—we're not even related! Historians think we are the result of breeding a Dachshund and an Italian Greyhound.)

Call me
Min Pin,
King of Toys!

Breed Buzzwords:
Energetic
Alert
Vigilant

If you were a Miniature Pinscher, here's what you'd think about:

FOOD!

I would appreciate a high-fat, high-protein diet. It helps me maintain my shiny coat and muscular build. Just because I'm small doesn't mean I'm not mighty.

GROOMING

I am naturally well groomed because my hair is really short. Every few days, I could use a quick comb to get rid of loose fur. But what's really great is a nice rub with a damp cloth afterward. (Make sure I'm dry before you take me outside.) And if you don't mind, trim my nails every few weeks, too.

EXERCISE

I am lap size but I am not a lap dog. Please, let me run! But make sure I can't escape, because I will if I can—and that can be dangerous. So fence me in or put me on a leash, but let me move!

TOYS AND STUFF

I like toys and lots of them. But do me a favor and get rid of little things lying around the house, like paper clips, because I might snack on them.

LEARNING TRICKS

If you're going to teach me, please be prepared with lots of tricks, because I'm a fast learner. Also make them exciting, daring, and fun.

MAKING FRIENDS

I suppose we can be friends, but don't call me too often and don't stand so close. I'll admit I'm a little suspicious of strangers. Have we met? Grrrrrr.

OBEYING THE RULES

I don't mind rules. I think rules are a good idea. Let's start with mine, and we'll get to yours later. Much later.

Shiba Inu

Average height:
14 1/4 to 15 1/2 inches
Average weight:
up to 25 pounds
Coloring:
red; red & white; white; white & black; black & tan; salt & pepper

Origins: We go way back to the seventh century in Japan. Today, there are more pet Shibas in Japan than any other breed!

What's mine is mine and what's yours is mine.

Breed Buzzwords:

Possessive!

Bold

Cute

If you were a Shiba Inu, here's what you'd think about:

FOOD!
I shouldn't get more than a cup and a half of food each day or I might get a little too plump. Here's the rule: You should be able to feel my ribs but not see them.

GROOMING
A good comb every now and then is always a good thing, but I don't need to do it every day. And give me a bath only when absolutely necessary.

EXERCISE
I could run for another hour or not. Whatever works for you. Because I'm small and catlike (don't tell anyone I said so), I get exercise just jumping around the backyard.

TOYS AND STUFF
They're mine. All mine. Everything is mine. But I'd rather chew on your fingers and toes than play with toys. Socks and shoelaces are good, too. But if you want to keep your things nice, then give me an old pair of socks tied in a knot or an old tennis ball.

LEARNING TRICKS
I'll learn a trick if you want me to, but would you mind if we made it seem like a game? Otherwise, I'm afraid I might get a little bored and start chewing on your stuff.

MAKING FRIENDS
My owner is my friend, my very, very, very best friend. All others, please fill out an application. If you want me to be really friendly, you should make sure I get used to other people and dogs when I'm just a puppy.

OBEYING THE RULES
I like to obey. If I see the neighbor's cat, though, I'm going to chase it. After all, I'm a hunter, have been for thousands of years.

Labrador Retriever

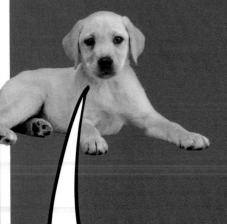

Average height:
21 to 24 inches
Average weight:
55 to 75 pounds
Coloring:
yellow; black; chocolate

Origins: We were originally from Newfoundland. We used to jump into icy water to pull the fishing nets ashore.

I was born to be your friend!

Breed Buzzwords:
Eager to please
Athletic
Cheerful

If you were a Labrador Retriever, here's what you'd think about:

FOOD!

I have one thing to say about food—YES, PLEASE! I'll eat whatever you have. I'm really active, so I need to keep up my strength.

GROOMING

I won't shed if someone brushes me on a regular basis (don't forget my undercoat). That is, I wouldn't shed much. I am a dog after all. It's part of my job to shed.

EXERCISE

Please don't let me go too long without running around outdoors. If you really want to make me happy, get me wet. I love to swim!

TOYS AND STUFF

In my opinion, there's nothing better than a toy you can throw and I can fetch. Balls and sticks are great! And no day is complete without a good chew on some rawhide . . . or your shoe.

LEARNING TRICKS

You know what I think is really fun? A good obstacle course—because I can follow the rules, run around, and work on my agility. But I'll do whatever you want. That's just who I am.

MAKING FRIENDS

I love friends. If someone isn't a friend, it's just because I haven't met them yet. I especially like children, and love living with a big family. Other animals are fine, too. Some of my best friends are cats. Maybe that's why we're the most popular breed in the United States.

OBEYING THE RULES

I aim to please (and I'm pretty smart, too). What I want most is to be your best friend. So tell me what the rules are and I will learn them—especially if they have anything to do with finding a duck or two.

Toy Poodle

Average height:
10 to 15 inches
Average weight:
6 to 9 pounds
Coloring:
any solid color

Origins: We started as water retrievers in Germany, where *pudd* means "one who plays in water." The fluffy poofs were originally to keep our joints warm when we swam.

Leave the grooming to the professionals! (Please.)

Breed Buzzwords:

Happy

Smart

Eager to please

If you were a Toy Poodle, here's what you'd think about:

FOOD!
A nibble here and a nibble there does the trick.

GROOMING
Don't even start with me about grooming! I need a trip to the groomer every six to eight weeks. Did you know that I'm not really French even though everyone calls me a French Poodle? I'm from Germany, but the French had so much fun making different shapes out of my coat that now everyone thinks France is where I'm really from! The French even consider me their national dog.

EXERCISE
I can live in the city or the country because the truth is, I really just need a daily walk. However, I prefer more. Here's what I really like—swimming!

TOYS AND STUFF
Show me something I can toss around and bark at, and I'll show you a good time! Remember, I've been a retriever for centuries, so think about toys that float.

LEARNING TRICKS
I don't want to brag, but there was a time (around the end of the eighteenth century) when you could find a Poodle act at almost any circus! That's because we like learning tricks and love to have fun.

MAKING FRIENDS
I like to think that I make a fine companion—charming, fun, and nice to look at. What more could you want?

OBEYING THE RULES
Just take a look at a dog show sometime! How many fine-looking Poodles do you see obeying the rules perfectly?

Miniature Schnauzer

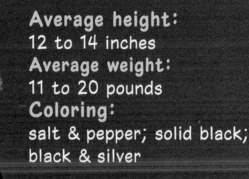

Average height:
12 to 14 inches
Average weight:
11 to 20 pounds
Coloring:
salt & pepper; solid black;
black & silver

Origins: We were bred in Germany in the 1800s to be a smaller version of the Standard Schnauzer. They were looking for a dog that could live in the house and catch rodents!

I'm no toy!

Breed Buzzwords:

Smart

Loyal

Lively

If you were a Miniature Schnauzer, here's what you'd think about:

FOOD!
I've got a lot of muscle, and that makes me sturdy, heavy, and sometimes pretty hungry! So I like to eat, but please don't feed me too much. When I'm an adult, I should weigh somewhere between 11 and 20 pounds.

GROOMING
Since I don't believe in shedding, I'm a great pet for people who are allergic to dogs. But I need to be combed weekly, and trimmed and cleaned every six weeks.

EXERCISE
I'll keep up with you if you want to run all day in the country, and I'm okay with staying home in a little apartment, too. What's more important to me is that I get to do whatever you're doing!

TOYS AND STUFF
I'm very good at catching rodents, so if you can find a little furry toy that runs across the floor, I would enjoy that. I also like sleeping with my family—save me a spot on the bed!

LEARNING TRICKS
I'm a quick learner. My best trick is hunting down mice, rats, and other little furry things that like to dive into holes in the ground.

MAKING FRIENDS
I love my family. I mean I *really* love my family. Friends are nice, but mostly I just want to do everything with my family.

OBEYING THE RULES
Ask anyone who knows me, they'll tell you—I'm very obedient. Many of my relations have done really well at formal obedience trials. We are a most well-behaved family.

Pembroke Welsh Corgi

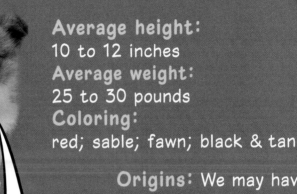

Average height:
10 to 12 inches
Average weight:
25 to 30 pounds
Coloring:
red; sable; fawn; black & tan

Origins: We may have been brought to Wales by the Vikings or the Celts thousands of years ago. *Corgi* means "dog" in Celtic. Either way, we were put in charge of herding the cows because we were good at dodging their kicks. It's easy when you're short.

I'll protect you!

Breed Buzzwords:

Devoted

Hardy

Smart

If you were a Pembroke Welsh Corgi, here's what you'd think about:

FOOD!

Since I'm not very tall and can weigh between 25 and 30 pounds, my back can start hurting pretty easily. So please don't overfeed me.

GROOMING

I don't like to spend too much time in front of the mirror. It's nice to get a brushing, but baths are really overrated. And as for shedding, I think it's important to do it twice a year.

EXERCISE

I don't need a yard if you don't mind my using the apartment for a playground. I need a good amount of exercise, but I'm good at getting it wherever I am. Although sometimes I can use a little encouragement to get moving since it's fun to spend the day on the couch, too.

TOYS AND STUFF

Who needs toys when you're the favorite breed of the queen of England?

LEARNING TRICKS

I'm not going to be jumping after Frisbees any time soon. But I'm so good at obedience that I can win competitions doing it!

MAKING FRIENDS

I am not a big fan of strangers, so if you want me to be nice, please start introducing me to other people and animals when I'm young. Also, just because I'm little doesn't mean I'm not an excellent guard dog.

OBEYING THE RULES

I know how to learn the rules because I'm smart. I'm also sensitive, so be gentle when you're telling me what you want. And while we're on the subject of behaving, I would like to say that I am very nice to children when they're very nice to me.

Do you think like a dog about FOOD?

Do you find yourself thinking . . .

I know I just ate but I'm starved!

Then: You can eat with the Labs!

Yeah, I'm hungry but did you just say, "play ball"? Let's go!

Then: You sound like a Shiba!

I wish dinner could just be left on the table so I could eat a little bit now, a little bit later, and a little more at midnight.

Then: We should invite you to a Toy Poodle party!

Do you think like a dog about GROOMING?

Do you find yourself thinking . . .

Hide! Mom wants me to take a bath!

Then:

I quite agree. Baths should be taken only when absolutely necessary.

I'm going to the beauty parlor. See you in three days!

Then:

Your style takes only three days? That's a walk in the park!

Then:

You should go to my barber. I don't have a bang problem, but try having a beard and eating from a bowl on the ground!

Hello? If I could see through the bangs, I would tell you if I needed a haircut or not.

Chihuahua

Average height:
6 to 9 inches

Average weight:
2 to 6 pounds

Coloring:
white; fawn; sand; chestnut; silver & steel blue; black & tan; parti-colored

Origins: We are from the State of Chihuahua in Mexico. But it seems as though Chinese travelers were the ones to take us from there and introduce us to the rest of the world in the late 1800s.

It's you and me forever!

Breed Buzzwords:

Courageous
Lively
Proud

If you were a Chihuahua, here's what you'd think about:

FOOD!

I'm the smallest breed in the world, so please don't feed me too much. Besides, I have enough other possible health problems to worry about, thanks to my short nose (wheezing) and prominent eyes (dryness and glaucoma).

GROOMING

When your hair is short like mine, you can just use a damp cloth as a brush. Although some of us do have longer coats, and they should be brushed every day. As for baths, once a month will do it, and please, please—don't get water in my ears.

EXERCISE

Okay, here's the thing—I'm tiny and cute, and you like to carry me and I like to be carried. But we both know that I'm going to be much healthier if you let me walk. Please put me in a harness, not a collar. They work better for us small folks.

TOYS AND STUFF

What I really need more than anything else is a nice collection of sweaters. I just hate cold weather, and nobody shivers more than I do. So feel free to dress me up and keep me inside! I am from Mexico, after all.

LEARNING TRICKS

I think my best trick is how fast I move when it looks like I'm about to get stepped on!

MAKING FRIENDS

My friend is my owner. My owner is my friend. I'm not so sure there's anyone else really trustworthy.

OBEYING THE RULES

I will obey rules if you ask nicely and not too often, but you should know it's hard to housebreak me. And, by the way, I'm not so good with children. I'm pretty delicate, and I get nervous and snappish around them.

Cavalier King Charles Spaniel

Average height:
12 inches
Average weight:
12 to 18 pounds
Coloring:
pearly white & red; white, black & tan; red; black & tan

Origins: King Charles II of England thought we were so great, he wrote a law that we be allowed in any public place, including Parliament. (That law still exists today!)

I ♥ sitting in laps!

Breed Buzzwords:
Gentle
Affectionate
Sporty

If you were a Cavalier King Charles Spaniel, here's what you'd think about:

FOOD!

I like a well-balanced diet, but please don't overfeed me. I gain weight really easily. Just feed me once a day and try not to give in when I ask for scraps—unless they're raw veggies. I like those and they're good for me.

GROOMING

Not only do you not need to trim my coat—you shouldn't! Please. My fur is long and silky and naturally wavy. And as if that's not cute enough, I have feathery fur on my ears, legs, feet, and tail. All I ask of you is a little brushing. I'll take care of the rest . . . including shedding.

EXERCISE

I get my best exercise getting on and off laps. But if you want me to move, give me something to chase. But make sure it's in a safe place. I'm smart, but not very streetwise.

TOYS AND STUFF

You know what's more important to me than toys and stuff? You. Please don't leave me alone for long, or I'll bark a lot and make a mess of your stuff.

LEARNING TRICKS

Is sitting on a lap a trick? I'm very good at that.

MAKING FRIENDS

I'm very peaceful and get along with most everyone. Just make sure you get me used to different people and animals when I'm young.

OBEYING THE RULES

I obey the rules except when I forget them. I can honestly say I did not mean to chew the pillow or bark at the neighbors or make that puddle in the living room. At least I always look cute. I also have a hard time not listening to my hunting instincts when I'm outside, so don't let me off my leash.

German Shepherd

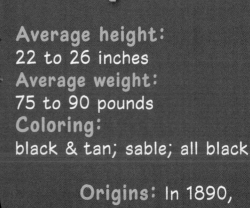

Average height:
22 to 26 inches
Average weight:
75 to 90 pounds
Coloring:
black & tan; sable; all black

Origins: In 1890, a German cavalry officer set out to breed a superb herding dog, using Germany's best farm dogs as the starting point. We are that dog!

Get a job!

Breed Buzzwords:
Stable
Intelligent
Loyal

If you were a German Shepherd, here's what you'd think about:

FOOD!
Please talk to my vet about how much I should eat, because labels on dog food often suggest too much. I'm counting on you.

GROOMING
Brush me. Regularly and thoroughly, please. And don't forget I have two layers of fur. The outer layer is dense, straight, and short. The undercoat is very soft.

EXERCISE
Please give me plenty of time and space to run every day. Did you know we were originally bred to trot all day long? We have excellent stamina.

TOYS AND STUFF
I prefer educational toys. (In other words, I'd rather have a job than a toy.) Life is always more fun when you're being challenged.

LEARNING TRICKS
I can do tricks if I'm not busy working. We do police work, tracking, guide work for the blind, bomb detection, herding, and avalanche rescue. Who has time to roll over and play dead?

MAKING FRIENDS
I'm good with kids. I'm part of the family, after all, and we all must take care of one another. In fact, we'd be better off if we just limited ourselves to family. I don't trust anyone else too much.

OBEYING THE RULES
You may call it "obeying the rules" if you like. I prefer to say I understand what is necessary to get the job done, and I work well with humans to achieve that goal. Got it?

Shetland Sheepdog

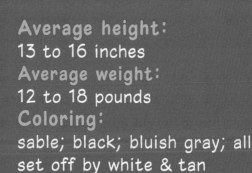

Average height:
13 to 16 inches
Average weight:
12 to 18 pounds
Coloring:
sable; black; bluish gray; all
set off by white & tan

Origins: We hail from
Shetland Island off the
coast of Scotland. That's
where we were bred to be
excellent all-round farm
dogs, guard dogs, and very
good friends.

Let's play!

Breed Buzzwords:
Hardy
Loyal
Obedient

If you were a Shetland Sheepdog, here's what you'd think about:

FOOD!

Don't trust the dog-food labels when it comes to how much to feed me. I'm not that big and don't really need that much to eat. Please keep the snacks to a minimum, too. Just like anybody else, I don't feel well when I'm carrying too much weight.

GROOMING

A weekly brushing would be most appreciated. But please do not clip my fur down to the skin—ever. However, you may trim the fur around my feet, ears, and legs. It can get a little long in those places. Also, if you don't mind, clean my ears.

EXERCISE

It's in my blood to run and herd. I love to run in wide-open spaces. Just be sure it's safe for me and that I can't get too far away.

TOYS AND STUFF

You might want to pick up a few balls and a Frisbee. I can really have a good time with a Frisbee.

LEARNING TRICKS

I could learn a trick, but I'd be happier if you would give me a job to do. If you don't have any cattle or sheep to herd, I could round up some of your pals. Just give me a job. Otherwise, I'm afraid I might start getting noisy and anxious, and neither of us wants that!

MAKING FRIENDS

I really like kids—especially if they're in my family. I love my family members and will protect them no matter what. Strangers, I'm not so keen on. But the more you introduce me to new people and places when I'm young, the better I'll be as a grown-up.

OBEYING THE RULES

We are herders. Herding dogs like to work and they like people. That means we're good at obedience, too. Go to any dog show and watch the obedience trials. I'll bet you'll see some Shelties in the group of high scorers!

Yorkshire Terrier

Average height:
6 to 7 inches
Average weight:
7 pounds
Coloring:
steel blue with tan head and legs

Origins: In nineteenth-century England, we were in charge of keeping rats out of coal pits and cotton mills. Since we're so small, we're really good at digging for rodents no matter where they try to hide.

Watch your step!

Breed Buzzwords:
Alert
Spirited
Inquisitive

If you were a Yorkshire Terrier, here's what you'd think about:

FOOD!
If I hit seven pounds, I'm as big as I should be. Please feed me accordingly. I also have a sensitive stomach and develop digestive problems easily. So no fancy treats. And please keep dry food in my bowl—it helps keep my teeth clean. (I get cavities very easily.)

GROOMING
You must brush me every day. It's my job to be soft and silky, and that doesn't happen without good brushing. Also, it would be great if you put a nice topknot on my head to get the hair out of my eyes. Here's the big bonus: I don't shed!

EXERCISE
I may be really tiny, but I still like to exercise. It doesn't take much. I can bounce around the living room and get a full workout.

TOYS AND STUFF
In my opinion, a sweater is always a good idea. I get chilly pretty easily.

LEARNING TRICKS
Like what? What could I do at seven inches high?

MAKING FRIENDS
Maybe we could just skip this section. I love my master, but all others please take one step back—especially little kids and other dogs.

OBEYING THE RULES
I'll be the first to admit it—I'm stubborn. But I'm still trainable . . . although I think housebreaking is really hard. Bottom line is this: I can do what you say, but mostly I would like you to do things for me instead.

Boxer

Average height:
22 to 25 inches
Average weight:
60 to 65 pounds
Coloring:
fawn; brindle

Origins: I have been used for a lot of different jobs in the past. I hunted, pulled carts, rounded up livestock, even worked as a circus dog. These days, we work a lot with police doing search and rescue.

I belong on the bed!

Breed Buzzwords:
Dignified
Independent
Protective

If you were a Boxer,
here's what you'd think about:

FOOD!

Okay—first off, I have to apologize for the drooling. It just happens when I'm around food. I would stop it if I could, but that's about as impossible as not snoring.

GROOMING

It's true we have short hair, but that doesn't mean we can't shed. In fact, we're really, really good at shedding. If you brush us every day during weather changes, you'll probably find less hair on your couch.

EXERCISE

Since I'm strong and active, please keep me involved in everything you do so I get plenty of exercise. Don't just put me in the backyard by myself, because I want you to play with me. I'm afraid, without you, I might get cranky.

TOYS AND STUFF

I love playing with toys, especially yours. I'm also a good boxer. I can jump up on my back legs and "box" with my front paws!

LEARNING TRICKS

Here are my tricks: barking, drooling, snoring, and shedding. I'm also really good at staying a puppy for a long, long time. We don't really mature until we're about four. But seriously, folks, we are actually really good at learning tricks.

MAKING FRIENDS

Here's the thing—just don't leave me by myself too much. Okay? I need to live in a house, with a family, and that's all there is to it. Otherwise, I'm afraid I might turn into a not-very-nice dog.

OBEYING THE RULES

If you stick with it for a long time and are very, very firm about what you want, I will think about working with you. But really, wouldn't life be easier if we just did things my way?

Do you think like a dog about EXERCISE?

Do you find yourself thinking . . .

I look okay, don't I? Why exercise when it's so comfortable here?

Then: It sounds like we have a few things in common. May I sit on your lap?

Exercise is part of a sound, healthy lifestyle. I can work out for hours and hours, and the more I do, the better I feel.

Then: It's a pleasure to meet someone who's smart and shares my point of view.

Exercise is around every corner. Seriously, I go around a corner and I feel exercised!

Then: You got that right! A corner can take a lot of time to turn if you're tiny. That's why they call it exerSIZE!

Do you think like a dog about TOYS AND STUFF?

Do you find yourself thinking . . .

Clothes are the best toy I can think of.

Then: ¡Si! ¡Si! Forget the bouncy ball and give me a sweater!

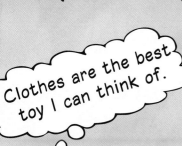

As long as it can be thrown, it's fun.

Then: We're a perfect match! You throw, I'll fetch!

Who needs toys for fun when you can run?

Then: Race ya!

Siberian Husky

Average height:
20 to 23 ¹/₂ inches

Average weight:
35 to 60 pounds

Coloring:
black & white;
gray & white;
red & white; white

Where's the snow?

Origins: We were originally from Siberia. We were brought to Alaska in 1909. We've been pulling sleds for as long as we can remember.

Breed Buzzwords:
Cheerful
Mischievous
Loving

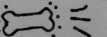
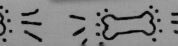

If you were a Siberian Husky, here's what you'd think about:

FOOD!

Since my breed is used to pulling sleds across Siberia, I know how to make the most of my food, and I don't need as much as you might think.

GROOMING

I don't need much grooming. But a thorough combing while I'm shedding is a really good idea. You'll be impressed at how much fur I carry around with me. That's why I don't think it's cold until it's about 58 degrees *below* zero. Oh! And please don't mess with the hair between my toes. I use it for gripping the ice.

EXERCISE

I need a good deal of exercise, so please think about fencing in the yard if you're going to invite me over. I might try to escape to find a good adventure. And while we're on the subject, please don't invite me over if it's too hot. I don't deal with heat very well.

TOYS AND STUFF

I like to chew as much as the next dog, so I wouldn't turn my nose up at a good chew toy. But mostly what I like to do doesn't need any extra stuff. I just want to RUN! I would love to be a jogging partner.

LEARNING TRICKS

Who needs to do tricks when you can run for miles pulling a sled in subzero weather?

MAKING FRIENDS

Please don't give me the job of watchdog. I always forget to bark and I never met a stranger I didn't like. Kids are swell, too. Actually, anyone is better than being alone. I want to apologize in advance for the things I destroy if you leave me alone. I just get so upset. Remember, I'm a sled dog. I like being in a pack.

OBEYING THE RULES

I will absolutely learn and obey the rules . . . as long as they make sense. But if I can't see the point in what you're saying, you might get the impression that I didn't hear you.

Beagle

Average height:
13 to 16 inches
Average weight:
20 to 25 pounds
Coloring:
tricolored red, white,
& orange; lemon & white

Origins: There are
accounts of packs of
hounds in England before
the time of the Romans.
The beagle didn't make
its way to America until
the 1860s.

Do you
smell
something?

Breed Buzzwords:

Gentle

Comic

Lively

If you were a Beagle, here's what you'd think about:

FOOD!

I want to make one thing perfectly clear: When I am hot on the trail of a rabbit or squirrel or the neighbor's cat, it's not because I'm hungry, it's because it's really fun to be hot on the trail of something that's running really fast! There's nothing—not even food—that I like better than a good chase!

GROOMING

I keep my coat close, hard, and not too long, so it doesn't take much to keep me looking my Beagle best. A weekly rubdown with a hound mitt or a brush with a firm bristle will do it . . . maybe a little more when I'm shedding. As for bathing, do that only when it's absolutely necessary. And use a mild soap.

EXERCISE

I'll follow my nose for miles and miles if I get hold of a good scent. I just can't stop myself. Someone really should fence me in so I don't wander too far away—although I will probably try to dig under the fence to escape.

TOYS AND STUFF

I like toys—balls, squeaky toys, chew toys. They're fun to toss around, and some of them are even good to sleep with.

LEARNING TRICKS

I would learn tricks if you could erase the smells that keep distracting me. Everywhere I go, I can tell you who's there, who's been there, or who's on their way! The nose knows!

MAKING FRIENDS

I just love children and other dogs. In fact, if you introduce me when I'm a baby, I'll even love a cat. I'm just a "get along" kind of dog. On the other hand, if I don't have a friend nearby, I might accidentally chew through the couch.

OBEYING THE RULES

I try hard to obey the rules, but there are certain things I have to do, like follow a scent and bark or howl at the slightest sign of danger or disruption. Sorry, but there's no way you'll get me to stop doing those things. You probably won't be taking me to any obedience trials, either.

Miniature Dachshund

Average height:
5 to 9 inches
Average weight:
up to 11 pounds
Coloring:
black & tan; reddish brown;
brindle

Origins: Hundreds of
years ago in Germany,
we were bred for hunting.
In fact, *Dachshund* means
"badger hound." We could
follow those badgers right
into the ground if we
had to! (We Mini Dachs
were good at hunting
rabbits, too.)

Oh!
My aching
back!

Breed Buzzwords:

Clever

Lively

Courageous

If you were a Miniature Dachshund, here's what you'd think about:

FOOD!

No matter what I say, do not give me more than two small meals a day. I will try hard to convince you I need more, but I don't. If I get too fat, I'll have a lot of back problems.

GROOMING

There are three different types of Dachshunds: Smooth, Wire-haired, and Longhaired. The Wirehaired and Longhaired dogs require more grooming than the Smooth. The Smooth just needs a rubdown with a damp cloth! You should also know that we Dachshunds are one of the few dogs that don't smell like a dog.

EXERCISE

I don't need a ton of exercise, but if I don't get about a half hour a day, I might get fat. Too much food and not enough movement can mean serious back problems for me. My favorite exercise is digging.

TOYS AND STUFF

Just make sure that whatever toys I have are not on the couch or up the stairs. It's not good for my back to jump up and down. A sweater or two would be nice for those chilly days.

LEARNING TRICKS

I hate to keep complaining about the same old thing, but whatever you want to teach me, please make sure it's not something that might lead me to spinal problems. A lot of Dachshunds end up with their hind legs in a little cart just to get around.

MAKING FRIENDS

If you leave me alone, I might bark a lot. Sorry, but it's in the genes. It makes me a great watchdog! As for other animals and children, I suppose if you introduce me when I'm very young, I might be able to be nice to them. But then again, maybe not.

OBEYING THE RULES

Not really my cup of tea, but thanks for asking. However, if you would like to obey my rules, that would be just fine.

Shih Tzu

Average height:
11 inches
Average weight:
9 to 16 pounds
Coloring:
black & white; brown & white

Origins: You can trace our family line back 2,000 years to China. We were part Lhasa and part Pekingese. *Shih Tzu* means "lion dog" in Chinese. We were often presented as very important gifts to Chinese royalty. Sometimes we were so pampered in the palaces, we were given human servants.

Don't hate me because I'm beautiful.

Breed Buzzwords:
Outgoing
Affectionate
Alert

If you were a Shih Tzu, here's what you'd think about:

FOOD!
You know the drill—little dog, little food. Otherwise, I will gain too much weight. That's a guarantee.

GROOMING
My coat is dense, long, and flowing. So please keep the brush ready . . . every day. And furthermore, please make a regular appointment with the groomer!

EXERCISE
Whatever. If you want to go for a little walk, I'll go with you, but I'm pretty content to stay on the couch.

TOYS AND STUFF
I don't really care so much about toys, although I do like a nice collection of bows and ribbons since I really need a topknot on my head if you want me to see where I'm going. (Or regular haircuts.)

LEARNING TRICKS
Don't ask me to do a trick. My job is to be a companion. I've been a house pet for about 2,000 years. In fact, in the old days back in China, I wasn't called a house pet—I was called a *palace pet!*

MAKING FRIENDS
I like people best—mostly full-grown ones. But well-behaved children are just fine with me, too. Actually, I also get along pretty well with other pets. Just don't surprise me or get me upset. Sometimes I nip a little when that happens.

OBEYING THE RULES
What rules? They never said anything about rules when I was in the palace. In fact, I'm the royalty around here, so shouldn't you be listening to me?

Golden Retriever

Average height:
20 to 24 inches
Average weight:
60 to 80 pounds
Coloring:
different shades of gold

Origins: We became popular in the 1800s in England and Scotland because we were such great hunters.

You can count on me.

Breed Buzzwords:
Friendly
Reliable
Trustworthy

If you were a Golden Retriever, here's what you'd think about:

FOOD!
Yes, please! And plenty of it. Okay. I'll admit it. I can get fat pretty easily, so maybe you shouldn't give me quite as much food as I want.

GROOMING
A little brushing and a bath now and then are about as much as it takes to keep me clean and fluffy. Thank you for asking.

EXERCISE
I don't like being too demanding but I really do need a yard so I can run around and get the proper exercise. By the way, if you were looking for something special I would like to do—take me to water. I LOVE to swim!

TOYS AND STUFF
Oh, boy! Do I love a good chew toy. Because nothing makes me feel worse than chewing up your shoes. See what happens when you leave me alone? Balls and sticks are great fun, too. In fact, anything that you can throw so I can fetch sounds like a good time to me.

LEARNING TRICKS
I don't like to call them tricks since I really like to spend my time doing things with a bit more meaning, such as helping the seeing-impaired. But on the other hand, if it's tricks you want me to do, then I'll do tricks. I live to please.

MAKING FRIENDS
No day is complete without children. I really like children. I understand they need patience and gentle handling. That's fine. Those are my specialties. There's nothing better than being part of a family, and that include lots of other animals, too.

OBEYING THE RULES
If I were feeling boastful, I might tell you about the obedience awards I've won, but I'm not boastful. I just want to be a good dog and do a good job—retrieving ducks, helping the seeing-impaired, tracking, or whatever my master wants.

Pug

Average height:
10 to 14 inches
Average weight:
14 to 20 pounds
Coloring:
black; silver;
apricot, fawn & black

Origins: We're one of the oldest breeds of dog, dating back as early as 400 BC! We probably started in Asia.

Love me, love my face.

Breed Buzzwords:
Even-tempered
Playful
Dignified

If you were a Pug, here's what you'd think about:

FOOD!

My problem is not that I become fat if I eat too much—I become obese! So, really, trust me when I tell you I will try to eat more food than I should.

GROOMING

My coat is fine, short, smooth, and glossy. A gentle brush is enough to make me shine! I would also really appreciate a few extra minutes from you to clean the creases in my face. As for baths, only when absolutely necessary. And I must be dried off right away—I get cold easily.

EXERCISE

If you could remind me every now and then to exercise, I would appreciate it. Sometimes it slips my mind, and the next thing I know, I've been on the couch for six days. But don't go nuts about it. I don't need tons of exercise, and please don't take me out when it's really hot or really cold.

TOYS AND STUFF

I like playing with toys, but nothing too strenuous, please. If I start to wheeze while we're playing, we should stop. I have chronic breathing problems, thanks to my short muzzle.

LEARNING TRICKS

Of course I understand what you want me to do, but it's just soooo boring to do the same thing over and over. And please don't shout. I'm very sensitive. If I'm not doing what you want, I'm probably just not interested, so shouting won't help. And it hurts my feelings. However, if we can reach an understanding, I'm actually pretty good at tricks.

MAKING FRIENDS

I'm happy to make room for others. Here's my list of possible friends: other dogs, pets, children, and visitors . . . but not if my owner spends more time with them than me. I'll admit I can be a little jealous.

OBEYING THE RULES

Again. Boring. But I will do what I can.

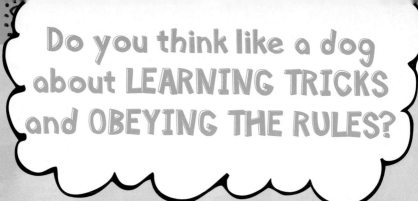

Do you think like a dog about LEARNING TRICKS and OBEYING THE RULES?

Do you find yourself thinking . . .

What's the point of all these silly games? Give me a job!

Then: I agree! Sign me up. I'll work for you anytime!

Yes, I hear you. I'm just not listening to you! Maybe I'll listen to you tomorrow.

Then: Oh, yeah! I hear that!

Take a look at the way I'm built. Just getting through the day is a trick!

Then: You can say that again!

Do you think like a dog about MAKING FRIENDS?

Do you find yourself thinking . . .

Then:

If I knew you, we might be friends. You seem like a nice person. But we haven't met, so I'm afraid I can't be nice to you.

You sound so much like me, I almost want to like you. But unfortunately I don't know you either, so I will have to bite you back.

Then:

Hear! Hear! I couldn't agree more!

Friends are fine, but family is everything.

Then:

I love you and you and you and you! Oooh! I just think everybody is fabulous!

Oh! Me, too! Me, too! May I sit on your lap?

45

THE OFFICIAL "THINK LIKE A DOG" QUIZ

1. You hear a strange noise in the middle of the night. You get up and run straight toward the noise and even when something kicks you backward, you come charging at the noise again. You won't stop for anything.

You are
a. a Miniature Dachshund
b. a Pembroke Welsh Corgi
c. a Labrador Retriever
d. all of the above

2. You are in your backyard when all of a sudden this unbelievably fine smell drifts past your nose. The next thing you know, it's getting dark, you've been running for a really long time, and you have no idea where you are.

You are
a. a Toy Poodle
b. a Golden Retriever
c. a Beagle
d. none of the above

3. You're standing in your kitchen, and everything you look at is yours. This makes you happy. Suddenly, someone else comes into the room and picks up one of your things. You are unable to hide your frustration. You like your things and you like others to understand that they are your things.

You are
a. a Shibu Inu
b. a Miniature Pinscher
c. a Shih Tzu
d. your little brother

4. You are home alone. Without meaning to, you discover that someone has left the closet door open, and the fifty-pound bag of dog chow is open and at ground level. You look both ways and then dive into the bag. You don't stop eating until it's all gone.

You are
a. a Shetland Sheepdog
b. a Chihuahua
c. a Labrador Retriever
d. none of the above

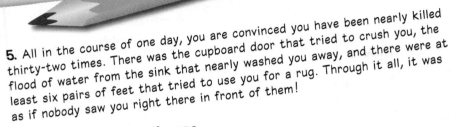

5. All in the course of one day, you are convinced you have been nearly killed thirty-two times. There was the cupboard door that tried to crush you, the flood of water from the sink that nearly washed you away, and there were at least six pairs of feet that tried to use you for a rug. Through it all, it was as if nobody saw you right there in front of them!

You are
a. a Yorkshire Terrier
b. a Pug
c. a Cavalier King Charles Spaniel
d. your hamster

6. You just spent the day working with the local police. Now you eat a quick meal before heading off to your night job as watchdog. Tomorrow, you will help a nice lady who can't see by fetching her groceries and running her errands.

You are
a. a Beagle
b. a German Shepherd
c. a Boxer
d. all of the above

7. It's January and you just can't get enough of the fresh air, so you head off on a light fifteen-mile run. Then, after a light lunch, you decide to do one more loop.

You are
a. a Chihuahua
b. a Toy Poodle
c. a Siberian Husky
d. your cat

8. You just came downstairs, which took quite a while, and now you realize you left your favorite sweater upstairs. You stand at the bottom of the stairs and wait for someone to come along to carry you because you know it could be bad for your health to climb the stairs too often.

You are
a. a Shih Tzu
b. a Shetland Sheepdog
c. a Miniature Dachshund
d. none of the above

ANSWERS

1.   b. Pembroke Welsh Corgi

2.   c. Beagle

3.   a. Shibu Inu

4.   c. Labrador Retriever

5.   a. Yorkshire Terrier

6.   b. German Shepherd

7.   c. Siberian Husky

8.   c. Miniature Dachshund

If you got:

4 or Fewer Correct Answers:
You're in the doghouse. Go back and read this book again!

5 Correct Answers:
You've made a good start at understanding how dogs think. Keep studying the dogs in your life and you'll be dog-thinking in no time.

6 Correct Answers:
You are making good progress, and no doubt the dogs in your life are pleased with your efforts.

7 Correct Answers:
Do you sometimes find yourself scratching behind your ears and chasing after bones? You are very clued in to dog-think.

8 Correct Answers:
How have you turned the pages of this book with your paws? Obviously, you are a dog.

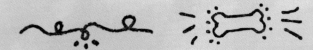